GAZE

Other Works by Christopher Howell

The Crime of Luck
Why Shouldn't I
Though Silence: The Ling Wei Texts
Sea Change
Sweet Afton
Memory and Heaven
Just Waking
Light's Ladder
Dreamless and Possible: Poems New and Selected

Limited Editions

The Bear in the Mirror
The Jetty
Red Alders in an Island Dream
The Wu General Writes from Far Away
Lady of the Fallen Air (from the Chinese)
King of the Butterflies

Anthology

Aspects of Robinson: Homage to Weldon Kees
(with Christopher Buckley)

GAZE
CHRISTOPHER HOWELL

POEMS

milkweed
editions

Published 2012 by Milkweed Editions
Printed in the United States
Cover and interior design by Hopkins/Baumann
Cover art by David Luckert. Reproduced with permission.
Author photo by Matthew Valentine
The text of this book is set in Berthold Garamond.
12 13 14 15 16   5 4 3 2 1
First Edition

Please turn to the back of this book for a list of the sustaining
funders of Milkweed Editions.

Library of Congress Cataloging-in-Publication Data

Howell, Christopher.
  Gaze : poems / Christopher Howell. -- 1st ed.
    p. cm.
  ISBN 978-1-57131-436-9 (acid-free paper)
  I. Title.
  PS3558.O897G39 2012
  811'.54--dc23
                                          2011029978

*This book is for John Somer
and the days of Kansas.*

Part I: View from the Afterlife

05 Home Stretch
06 Gaze
07 First Touch
10 Long Arm of the Lake
12 My Mother and the Sky
13 Four Prodigals in the Afterlife
15 Dinner Out
16 A Lump of Coal
17 Asylum: The Morningside Hospital Farm for Eskimos Driven Mad by Change
19 Geography Lesson
20 Twenty Years Apart
21 The Moment Before a Change
22 Hammer
23 Greenhouse Sparks and Snow
24 After the Afterlife

Part II: The Other Life

29 All of Us Are Dreaming
30 The Circular Saw Children Confess Their Joy
31 Being Read
33 Brothers Find Each Other in the Dark
34 The House Was Not Our House
36 Rain Sanctorum
37 The Day the Field Burst into Flame: Another View
39 Checkers
40 Candle: A Christmas Tale
42 At Sea
44 Tale of the Attempt to Return Our Separation
48 The Story
49 Rachel
53 Three Voice Roulette at Ghostly's
55 The Rain Is Not Discouraged
56 Bon Voyage

Part III: The Inner Life (With Crows)

61 The Inner Life
62 Report from the Empty Room
64 The Refusal to Count Beyond Seven
65 The Paradox of Place
66 Twine
67 After Three Years
68 Elinor
69 The Agnostic Prays for Rain
70 Wind off the River Asks if I've Seen
    Myself Lately, and, if so, Do I Remember the Name
72 A Crow's Elegy for the Farmer's Daughter
73 Cascade
75 De Pictura
76 Una Furtiva Lagrima
77 The Mystery of Names
78 I Wake Again
79 Listen

Acknowledgments

Thank you to the editors of the following publications, in which many of the poems in this volume originally appeared: *American Literary Review, Artful Dodge, Ascent, Basalt, Bellingham Review, Beloit Poetry Journal, Crazyhorse, Field, The Gettysburg Review, Hanging Loose, The Hampden-Sydney Review, Hubbub, Knockout, Lit Rag, Lyric Review, New Ohio Review, Northwest Review, New Orleans Review, Prairie Schooner, Redactions, Rock & Sling, The Southern Review,* and *Third Coast.*

Additionally, some of the poems have been anthologized as follows.
"Dinner Out," *180 More Extraordinary Poems for Every Day,* ed. Billy Collins (New York, NY: Random House, 2006).
"First Touch," *Long Journey: Contemporary Northwest Poets,* ed. David Biespiel (Corvallis, OR: Oregon State University Press, 2006).
"Gaze," *Breathe: 101 Contemporary Odes,* eds. Prevost & Van Cleve (Chattanooga, TN: C & R Press, 2008).
"At Sea," *Alhambra Poetry Calendar 2009,* ed. Shafiq Naz (Bruges, Belgium: Alhambra Publishing, 2009).
"Greenhouse Sparks and Snow," *Poets of the American West,* ed. Lowell Jaeger (Kalispell, MT: Many Voices Press, 2010).
"Cascade" appeared on the *Poetry Daily* website (eds. Boller & Selby).

I wish to thank the Washington Artist Trust and the Eastern Washington University Research and Creativity Committee for fellowships which helped make completion of this book possible. Special thanks also to David Luckert, Melissa Kwasny, and Christopher Buckley for their generous and intelligent commentary, and for their steadfast friendship.

GAZE

PART
I
VIEW FROM THE
AFTERLIFE

And if you should die, are you not certain
of reawaking among the dead? Let yourself
be carried along, events will not tolerate your
interference. You are nameless. The
ease of everything is priceless.
André Breton

Home Stretch

I'm coming home, but it's a long way. In fact
when I finally arrive they'll be snapping
my picture and shrugging it all over the neighborhood's
raised eyebrows, calling me *That One Who Only
Resembles*. Every few minutes someone will ask,
"Can I help you?" But I'm coming home, mud and birdsong
buttering my blamelessly cloud-like steed, saddlebags
weeping with souvenirs from "Beyond the world," surely.
Surely I'll be home to my sparrow bone memory house
shaking its flags of welcome like the unknown
language of judas trees calling an empty room
to attention. Eventually the mayor will want to know
what I've forgotten and just who do I think he is?
And I'll put on a beautiful headdress and walk out
on the lily pads, just as I always incredibly intended.
I'll keep saying, "Receive me. Here are my silver
wings, in accordance with custom. Inside of them
leaves have been falling all these years."

Gaze

I gaze through glass
at the red maple by the garage
and the bird feeder

empty of birds.
What is the meaning of life?
Cisco and Pancho are laughing

as they ride, flinging back
their sombreros. The ridiculous
and somber Lone Ranger

fills me with love.
My mother walks through wind
to the clothesline

and I am happily no one
I need to know
trotting up the path

between orchards in a blue
cowboy hat.
I gaze again. The clouds are silver

stallions above foothills of the Cascades
east of us. There's my mother
again, leaning down to pet the dog,

straightening, shading her eyes
to view the clouds, a stampede
of laundry-like meaning

at which she shrugs.

First Touch

After the movie, the garden golf,
coffee, and long soulful walk,
after the alternating daisy petals
of elation dejection elation, we stood
in the klieg lights on her front porch.
I could hear through the door
the ox-like breathing of her father
poised to fling it wide and pounce.
From the roundness of her green eyes
I could tell she heard it too.

But inside us some kind of execution
was on the way, and we were its last meal,
our mouths beginning to know this
and to open, slightly and drift toward each other
like clouds.

We had been kissing for months.
This kiss was not that
country, this one
had nothing to do with gratitude
or the sort of evening we had had
or expectation
or revenge against parents and the church
or even curiosity.
It was the exclusivity of desire, the dizzy
mutually sudden focus of our young neurons
driving us onto a single unrepeatable moment
of physical revelation fused to a steam
of lips and tongues and interpenetrating breath.

When at last we disengaged from that
eternity, still
holding me, she turned her back to the door, took
my hand and, in a gesture ceremonially exact, placed it
upon her breast.
She was wearing a bra, a blouse, a sweater
and a coat. She might have been Joan of Arc

arrayed for battle.
Nevertheless, the magnitude of this gift
surged up my arm, neck, and into my hair
till I began to lift
or faint
and felt the moon raking my blood with gems.

She drew away, smiled a little, and opened the door.
Her father, standing like Stonehenge
against the living room light, allowed her in
then shut the whole house, hard, the lion-headed
brass knocker banging like a gunshot.

I moved throbbingly down the steps and headed home.
After a block or so I could walk
normally. The softness of her lips and tongue,
that roundness and tension beneath my palm
as she held it to her, every step
brought these and such a warm loneliness
came over me, I thought I would not much mind death
then, if gods *could* die.

I walked down Hawthorn Street from 82nd to 89th
through a hall of overhanging trees, through the small
kivas of light that fell from the streetlamps.
Did I continue on Hawthorn to 92nd
or turn left and cross the dark school yard?
It was a long time ago. Kennedy was President; Viet Nam
just a place we sent "Advisors."
Moths were circling the porch lights and dying
in ecstasies of brilliance.
No one in the world but her
knew where I was.

Long Arm of the Lake

When I was ten,
we rented a cabin by a lake so deep
no one knew
what might drowse in its dark body.

The place was drafty
and my father fought for hours
with the stove, finally
settling for a fire out under the amazed
starlight where we roasted hotdogs
and devoured them like fire eaters
right off the sticks.

It was wonderful
but behind me I could feel huge wings
of a spirit
moving near us through the rippling dark.

Later, in the chill of my Army surplus sleeping bag,
I thought it might be a kind of crow, one of the gods
of hatred, living there, feeding
on what we couldn't help
but be, and coming for me especially
on account of my having smashed
Bobby Stricker's nose
with my lunch box
and spent not a single moment
in contrition for this act,
the hate therefore still breathing as I breathed, happy
with the jaunty angle of its hat.

All night I lay in terror of the lake
fifteen feet away.
All day in the leaky boat I fished for strength
and helped my father spool and respool the nightmare
tangles his ancient casting reel kept serving up.
As we headed in, gratefully, at five,
my mother on the shore, waving, relieved
and brimming with false cheer,
my pole bent double and I found myself
too tired to care
about whatever version of the Devil
my hook had caught. I reeled it in, a five-pound bass,
flopping and miraculous,
and beat its brains out on the stern
just as I'd been taught.

My Mother and the Sky

I think of my mother
bending above a pot of flowers.
Are there bees in there?
The blue sky hums, so maybe.

Along the street sleepy cars
begin plotting the day's error.
What does my mother care?
She has her clippers.

Birdsong birdsong birdsong spills
from the lilacs my mother once
placed at an edge of the world
she wanted, precisely.

I think of my mother dreaming
a pot of flowers and the day
they must become an absence of all
but one affection, birdsong

bending
because of lilacs, my mother and the sky.

Four Prodigals in the Afterlife

I.

The hour leans, and why not
see the shape of someone whitening an absence
or a door?
Even the roofline buzzards coo and clack: surprise!
we're back!
Beyond the fence posts, out of sight
the years have whispered off like flames,
struck still numbers, fading names
left along the trail to steer us right.

II.

An iron claw. A place to stand and fail
as light must fail. These nothings are the law
of sudden rock. Truth is
we have been long upon the trail
of this disaster, this smile of stove in boats
and grit along the shore. Does everyone
come home at last
to ruin? Tarnished brass fragments lie about
like old crimes among the weeds' repast.
The beloved are missing and presumed. Breeze
flails in acres of wrecked Chevrolets and ruts.
So at last we have returned. Is this the end

III.

or a beginning? Either way, what form pertains
when sun declines to serve
and waking traps its secret master like a slave? Either way
life must be the sum. So it may be even robins have come back
and the mountain, if there is one, hums
with bees. Imagine a morning more
beautiful
if you can: the prince absorbed in singing
as the curtains of his chamber sway like women dreaming
in a dream. This is a truth: white birds
are piping in their trees
as though they know our secret
and they do.

IV.

There is no need to celebrate
shadows of the reeds. The eyelid
moon's arrival. Child of a stranger's day that lasts and lasts.
Among the tides of rhododendron and phlox
heavens perish and appear, we are there
so briefly. We are here. So long.

Dinner Out

We went to either the Canton Grill
or the Chinese Village, both of them
on 82nd among the car lots
and discount stores and small nests
of people waiting hopelessly
for the bus. I preferred the Canton
for its black and bright red sign
with the dragon leaping out of it
sneezing little pillows of smoke.
And inside, the beautiful green
half-shell booths, glittery brass encrusted
lamps swinging above them.

What would I have?
Sweet and sour?
Chow mein with little wagon wheel shaped
slices of okra and those crinkly noodles
my father called deep fried worms?
Fried rice?

Among such succulence, what did it matter?
We could eat till we were glad and full, the whole
family sighing with the pleasure of it.
And then the tea!
All of this for about six bucks, total,
my father, for that once-in-awhile, feeling
flush in the glow of our happy faces
and asking me, "How you doing, son?"

Fine, Dad. Great, really, in the light
of that place, almost tasting
the salt and bean paste and molasses, nearly
hearing the sound of the car door
opening before we climbed in together
and drove and drove
though we hadn't far to go.

A Lump of Coal

I wasn't sure I heard her, at first,
because of the wind
with everything in it, textbooks
and ice cream and chinchillas
and stars made of paper and glitter
          and glue.

She was standing by the school, crying
with the hurt someone had delivered
like the bad gift a mean boy
brought to a birthday party once
when I was twelve
          and had walked

halfway up the mountain to get there
in time for cake. I remember
the unwrapping, the glistening spheroid
shadow shedding dust,
and then the silence and the tears
          descending

just as from this girl in blue
leaning against the school gym not so many
years later on, when I had grown disdainful of weeping
and of those who wept, who let their books
fall like small, useless bricks and turned their beautiful
          blond heads aside

and would not be comforted. And when at last
I touched her, blackbirds flew from her thin
wrists and up
over the row of swaying and choir-like poplar trees
to where nests would keep their young ones
          from the likes of us.

Asylum: The Morningside Hospital Farm
for Eskimos Driven Mad by Change

Morning or evening at the east edge
of the orchard
where a wire fence leaned against the grass
we might see them dazed
in blue pajamas
as they tended their herd of listless Guernsey's,
in the course of which, sometimes,
                        they wandered
clear to the fence line and stared into us
as though we were distance
or fog
and they water
lapping a rocky beach, though it was Portland
in the Fifties, miles from the sea.
                    What therapeutic scheme
had sent them south
into our rainy and alien greenery, no one asked
or knew.
            When one or two, almost by accident,
would scale the wire and find themselves
among our peach trees, silent men in white
materialized
and dragged them, with purgatorial kindness,
back
to the fields of their nether life.
                        Many times, on Sundays
as we passed by
on our way to church,
                    an old man
in a bathrobe paced the verge of Stark Street, just
outside the gate, weeping,
bent, hysterical, amazed,

in the indifferent two-lane roar of a world
that was not the world, his mouth shivering like a trap
as it opened
and snapped.

Others,
in their ill-fitting pajamas, rocked
on benches or stood
by the curb, weeping and shouting like ice
breaking up,
sweeping downstream in a gesture
                              of no return.

    *   *   *   *

Now, for more than thirty years, their pasture
is a parking lot
and mall, all trace of the perfect
park-like grounds and pale frightening buildings
erased.
Where did they go, the hollow-eyed
hundreds? How far
this time
were their ghosts made to walk?

    *   *   *   *

On a clear night, sometimes,
we would hear, drifting over fields from the dormitories,
a many-voiced, ravaging, all
too human fugue, a lost wind rising
and falling,
searching the universe for snow.

Geography Lesson

Was it true you could walk to Tierra del Fuego
if you felt like it? Mrs. Edmiston
in her pink shoes and glittery horn-rimmed
glasses behind which her eyes were
like blue fried eggs
looked out the second-floor window
of Marysville School and said it was.
And from Point Barrow, with a good telescope,
you could see the Communists
yearning to breathe free, collectively, though they
hated God, as Krushchev's behavior
clearly indicated. But if you did go south

of course you'd have to ford the Panama Canal
and watch out for snakes and man-eating
fish all the way through the Amazon, to say nothing
of head hunters, poison darts, and diseases
that could turn you into a heap of smoking jello.
But you *could* do it. Americans, she told us,
were both free and brave, as
opposed to those who lived elsewhere
and were naturally slothful, cunning, cowardly,
deceitful and generally unevolved.
Also the longest river in the world was the Nile
in Africa, the dark continent with its gorillas
and lions and savage tribes (who wore either no
underthings or nothing *but* underthings)
and diseases so horrible, well,
she didn't even want to *talk* about them.

How fortunate we were! She tapped
the blackboard pointer against her palm and said,
Is there anyone here who doesn't know
how fortunate he is?

Twenty Years Apart

The light of our arms distresses us
as it flings itself away from its sleeves.

I remember cows in a field of blue maize, their faces
dancing the cow wedding dance.

Some fragments of springtime bred in the shade
of a night fisherman, whistling.

I remember the smile of a grey wagon at dusk
as it did nothing among the wildflowers.

All over the island, lamps came on like jars
with old men inside them, lighting their pipes.

I remember how we sat on a stump above the harbor
naming the heavens, letting our own names go.

The Moment Before a Change

In shallows, among reeds and notes
of the troubled lilies,
I am uneasy.
The yellow mouth of the moon is shut.
A grey glow comes upon the world again

and again it is Mercer Lake in 1955
when I crept out of the rented cabin
and saw the huge black angel bathing,
hard pewter-like pieces of lake
falling from his wings.

I gave some of my eyesight
and most of what I had been hoping for
as a bribe that he might bless me
and he gave me an onyx lens
to hold against the change of light
and its bread
bumping darkly under layers of mist.

All common prayer is uselessness
when memory dresses and descends
into you, leaving doors ajar
and immense fir trees and mirror-like alleyways
of fallen shelves everywhere you step.

I know you, it says,
you're the one who stands reed-still
under new stars and the old ones
with their faces turned away,
the one who's uneasy, who remembers
and hasn't quite paid.

Hammer
for Dev Hathaway

It's the same one my grandfather
threw off the roof
after smacking his thumb.
Heft it and you might see it still
tumbling like a re-entering satellite
through the butter-colored birdsong
of spring, its hard ears
cocked as if hearing the *look out!*
that follows it, spitting out nails
and sending six shingles
into the tops of nearby trees. Maybe

you even see it coming
like you're nine years old and in love
with ladders and the magical clink
and thud and silver shine of tools.
Beyond it, too, perhaps you glimpse
the horrified faces, mouths open
like zeros, eyebrows way up
toward the bills of those once white
snap-down caps as you catch
with a cherubic juggler's grace
this hammer
and pray you might be given
to bear it all the way back
up each sacred rung
to where the gods, who will never die,
are repairing the roof of Heaven.

Greenhouse Sparks and Snow

It is night and my grandfather potters around, grafting
various geraniums to other geraniums, goading to life
brilliant hybrids to amaze the window boxes
of his cadre of aging customers, and for the fun of it.

He has fired up that potbellied stove
my parents will later turn into a planter
and through the stovepipe chimney sparks dizzy up
toward the stars like a kind of interstellar spawn
going home.

The old man looks up, though he cannot have heard
my footfall on the path that passes through the orchard
from his house to ours, or the light tapping I can't resist
bringing to the glass.

Pipe in his mouth, he makes another cut, mating stranger
to stranger with the unhurried precision that comes
with a lifetime of presiding over floricultural weddings
of this kind.

The stars turn. He does not look up again, though
I think hard to bring his peaceful face
into my room, four hundred miles and forty years
away.

What have I made of myself? He would want to see
the garden
and to try out the chair I sometimes, on nights like this,
edge up to the fire. The news in general
would not interest him and he would puzzle

at my sadness as I try to say how much he is
my own life
of sparks and snow and stars but also work and, here and there,
love's mortal blossom.

After the Afterlife

Swallows dip by the blue of a nameless
window.
Bits of St. Bridgid's roses begin their dream of her

intimately beyond dust, another sort of blossom
tending itself and looking up as the bride descends an iron stair
thinking, "hammered silk, what could be

more beautiful?"
Charles says something about the love of death, that thing
in us that gathers behind a door.

Please me and let me go, I think.
Reach me
a black wing to solve that house where old stars burn

and beckon and call out
that they knew Jesus long ago, that he was a form of wonder.
Reach me a hand or silver rope

for my return.

PART
II
THE OTHER LIFE

Old ghost, friend of this house, remain!
What is there now to prod us toward
The past, our ruinous nostalgias?
Weldon Kees

All of Us Are Dreaming

Outside the jail rain is musing down
a street that simply ends.
Beyond, in the blue hills, three horsemen
ride furiously toward town
but draw no nearer. Their faces
are wooden concealments and their hats
are wrong—born
under the wrong stars, some would say.

Inside the jail an old bandit
builds himself out of leather

and hope. Sometimes he sings "Don't
Fence Me In" in a voice like bent nails.
When the Sheriff's daughter comes with muffins
on a tray, the bandit's loneliness and lust
lead him to such age
he disappears, and she sets down her offering
in front of the emptiness
and says, "I brought this for you."

The Circular Saw Children
Confess Their Joy

We waited, of course, to become disks
as the sun and moon

and Mother's mirror. We thought
it would be perfect to be endless
edges gliding, perhaps flung
and cutting things off at the knees.

The cruelty of such circumstance
would not belong to us
but to the shape of us
merely, an accident of science
or a miracle or fate, as, say a sudden
bright blue rose rising like a cobra
beside a white gate.

We thought doilies, lids, and portholes
were our secret sins
wheezing in the hallway's dream
of flattened hats and all things orbital and thin
enough never to grow old.

We imagined the face of our round lake
a god or djinn
demanding sacrifice, which is why
we tied and threw our neighbor in.

"Don't worry," we said to his disappearing frown,
"what's drinking you, that perfect 'o,'
will make you one of us as you go down."

Being Read

And then the pale book opens
just as a man turns
his own page

calling, "Is anyone there?"
the green umbrella
of his question unfolding

against the night falling in pieces
around his footsteps
that make no sound, he is so alone.

Is he a glass of water, the just out of reach
thumb
of a retired blacksmith's imagination?

As he approaches his door
out of courtesy
it sings to him. His key begs to be held.

Inside he places the umbrella
in its answerless corner
and lends his hands to a bowl

of something he asks for
and quietly
asks again. You can hear him

in the book he offers
so you'll know those leaves
and empty windows

and women combing their hair everyplace
else in the world
form no part of his intention,

that he had meant to turn a different page
and step
into his true and wordless body.

Brothers Find Each Other in the Dark

The sleep of likeness brings these brothers on,
shoulders sloping the same, eyebrows arched exactly
and then the same
dreamy glow about them as they move
slowly
among the multitudes, hands in scuffed pockets,
and looking around.

A barker calls, "Hey, take a chance, now,
take a chance."
The brothers stroll on [what chance?] more and more
the same, the ghost of their separation closing
invisibly.

At a shout from somewhere behind them
they turn, perfect as dancers who have become a waltz
of acceptation, mildly surprised to find themselves
unsurprised by this unity of gesture, this bell-like longing
that does not ring.

Supple is one word for how they are tonight
among the organ grinders and the lights, party boats aglimmer
on the lake.

Wander turn step and turn. They find the world
far stranger than they knew, but comforting. A song they used to
     sing
drifts to them exactly like a thing that isn't there.

The House Was Not Our House

but we stopped there and my father said
"No one move," as the black glass door swung
toward us on its creaking hinge.
"It's a sign," he said, and then again, "No one move."
I saw above the great brick turret a banner
bearing a winged green device.
A kind of whistling drifted down off the roof.
In the open doorway stood only the lightless room
beyond.
   Why are we here, I wondered.
Then a man came out and wrote in chalk
upon the doorsill, "COLLECTIONS."
   Father
stepped down from the carriage and went in, walking
stiffly upright.
We never saw him again.
The sky was the color of chalk for years.
We kept returning to that place. Each time
one of us would go in, looking for the others.
      Finally
I rode alone up the long drive, my heart in a dish,
all my life coming on
behind me like a string of penitents,
      or soldiers
whose enemy had vanished and left them nothing
to do but go home.
    When I knocked, something beautiful
from the past said, "This is not your house, not yet."
So I turned everything around, led the whole parade
back, and now I have my father's voice each time I pray
and my absent sisters deliver me their rings
and pearl inlaid combs. Clearly
they desire congress with the monster of chalk
and collections.

I do not know where he is
but feel his breath collect us one by one
and yet remain somehow lonely as a journey that goes on

until even the blind forget their dark
suffrage or the seventy-two names of God
climb off the wheel and write themselves in dust.

Often, though I do not speak, my own voice
says, "Why are we here? It's a sign! No one move!"

It was
a huge old house, its grey stone lintels
glistening with wet. In its courtyard ten thousand carriages
burned with the moon's chalk-white milk.

Rain Sanctorum

In a high corner a face of rain turns
as if, after years of pink drought
and sheep flying unnaturally, uncountably,
over sleep's fences
in search of the drowsy soul, the world
wanted it again.

And near the door the door imagines
itself
and the left-handed brass latch laughs
like a fried component
of something uselessly wakeful on a shelf
in a room in another world
brilliant with old men
walking by the brilliant sea.

What now?

The face of rain offers its pale eyes,
the room is more and more sleepily
shivered in secret lace
which it slowly unbuttons.

What now?

The Day the Field Burst into
Flame: Another View

I think of old Mrs. Johanssen walking past
on her journey to and from the store each day
at dusk, and my mind follows the shadows behind her
thrashing as though the sudden trees were running
for their lives

as we had run
up onto my grandmother's porch
for shelter that day in 1951. Could you see this
picture, you might see too the huge
field of weeds and scotch broom
explode, a great hammer of smoke and flame rising
to smite the neighboring fields, Mrs.
Johanssen throwing both shopping bags
over her head and sprinting like a supersonic gnome.

You might turn as we did and find God
right there
playing pinochle with the others, calling out
the tricks and trumps until a wild
wind of blue-tinged rain slashes out of the west
soaking the firemen and the fire
coughs and dies
and He says, "See?"

An estimable sleep may have reached us all
after that. If we are nothing
but this sleep, how
should I know? I'm mortal and was dying
to believe
in the fearless man who sees the form of God

blur and diminish as it moves off
down the path between the orchard and slouching
barn, and who all his life thinks of this
darkening blue outline as something
inside himself that remains
calm
even as flames roar and grin and he's six years old
again and again.

Checkers

Jesus and Buddha lean above a checker board.
Each moves the other's invisible pieces,
though, from a certain point of view, the game
neither begins nor ends.
Pearls fall from the nacreous clouds.
Behind them on the wall is the perfect
outline of a parking meter
and a bird shaped like the number five
to indicate that five of everything remains,
including five realities, in each of which someone is
asking, "Why pay more?" a question the players
move between them like a shuttle on a loom,
Buddha occasionally asking, "Why pay at all?"
and Jesus answering, "Everybody pays."

Candle: A Christmas Tale

She lived behind the hag-like curtains in the dust of that
immense and blackened house.
At midnight, we whispered, her eyes lit up in flame
    and her sighs
scraped along the nearly endless hall, down
the stairs, through iron fingers of the door latch and
    out the gate
to which, surely, every child who passed too slowly by
would be lashed for later roasting. We believed
    these things completely.

The woman was so horrible with loneliness, we imagined
with a kind of exquisite zeal
the lover said to have gone off to war (in maybe 1812,
    we thought)
and her years of patience
overcoming, room by room, the house until there was nothing
but herself, rattling
among the knickknacks and darkened windows of her loss.

This did not explain why she was said to strangle rats
as well as children
and eat them slathered in fifty-year-old strawberry preserves,
    but it made
the monstrousness of her suffering
horrid and beautiful as a bowl of blackened rubies,
    each placed carefully
with the others
by a boney ringless lace-cuffed hand.

On Halloween she might be heard to sing while weeping, if one
    dared to listen.
At Christmas we would sneak out to see the single candle
peering all night from her third-floor window with such lonely
    malice
we almost understood the birth of Christ,
at last, as a matter called forth by the strangenesses of selves
in their eachness and burning and the cold night close around
    us all.

"Jesus!" we whispered, thinking of death and resurrection, of wise
    men and cows,
of those who had heard angels once and then stood waiting, in
    agonies of perfect faith, among the hills.

At Sea

Somewhere near Tenerife we saw the Northern Lights
pulsing and arcing, a blanket of iridescence shaken out
      in the wind.

Some of the old hands said it was a bad sign
to see The Lights over your left
      shoulder

because that's where death sits, smiling and smoking
his foul cigars, though maybe that was just
      a thing they said

to make our meat creep and I knew that about death
anyway. They also said The Lights and the blue
      white phosphorus

almost bright enough to read by were twin brothers
separated at birth and placed somehow in the world
      of distances

like time, that is, like something you can't fool
or bargain with.
      Flying fish kept leaping

with astonishment into the strange night. We found
them flopping all over the deck, glittering with
      phosphorus, mad

about the sky, and unsuspecting as we scooped them up.
I remember Isaacssen saying it was all right
      to eat them:

they were probably Communists. We never knew
what he meant by that. The Lights followed us
    for days and the fish

followed The Lights. And the phosphorus kept arguing
its point about the reliability of salt, as though
    Reason mattered.

Tale of the Attempt to Return
Our Separation

I.

By the condition of that smile shining
from the cavern of his helm, we could tell
the sentry had been dead a hundred years.

Nevertheless we edged
past him like the shadows
of shadows
and entered a courtyard where thousands
of sleeping dogs yipped and growled
according to the struggles of their dreams.

High in the stone face of the keep, curtains
ghosted from staring sockets of the order
of primal defense as we began

to climb the spiraling stair
like a penitential delegation of the righteous
on its way to Heaven to complain about
the food
or the inconstancy of blessing.

At length we entered a room of bones and jewels
and women bathing in a kind of glittering dust.
We gave them our swords and arrows,
the rings from our cold right hands, and bowed
to the priceless platinum sheen their bodies made.
At last our mission had become
clear to us.

So we gathered what bones we could
and went on
up a darker stair, leaving the diamonds
and rubies and women, their beauty and dust, for someone
else, for the dogs and sentry
should they wake. We simply kept
climbing
our desire, cradling
the anonymous dead
like so many ivory harps borne toward a fugue
of nameless unendurable finality and precision.

In one of the upper galleries, a man's head
encased in glass screamed calmly about *vertu;*
and in the niche of a narrow turning we found a nest
of half-burnt candles
left by those whose courage brought them only
so far
and went out.

Ill omens, yet we had hope.

Our armor
rang in the black sleeve of the tower
and we heard, tolling as if for the first time,
a gladness of judgment which left war to others
and set us to the great work of redeeming something
lost
that was not ourselves.

Who were we to become such men?
At first we were many
and then there were the same few there have always been
to carry the world's bones,
to give them back.

II.

The journey became a choir
of invisible strangers, but at each turning the absence
of any indication of a sign
renewed our desire to see it through.
Ortega said it was well
we had declined to heed the screeching head
of Robespierre, that purely mad beacon
of the broken ring.

He said thus by our continuance we must become
a flight of prelapsarian angels
married, at last, to the absolute.
Then he fell down dead and smiling, one more
stranger beside the path.
As a sheerly practical matter, we turned away, each
into his own thought, which we knew
Ortega would be listening for.

Next it was Cairns,
who had spoken again and again
of the Virgin
alphabet, that singing we sometimes suspected
inside the furious grey nonchalance of the stones
through which we moved, bearing
our little lamps of hopefulness.

He stood suddenly still, pointed to his heart
and said Remember this, this is the ship
of sky and wind above your house
when you were small, and the dirt road
and the field and the dream you had of Heaven.
This is the drum of the soul.
Then he lifted, incredibly, above us like a veil or message
borne off by breeze into the afternoon
leaving us too surprised to bid him well,
though I, since I am the last,
do so now.

III.

I say I am the last
and yet, who knows? We searched
for God in order
to return, like an overdue book, this greatest gift,
death, that it might sustain
and please Him
as it has ourselves
by clothing the infinite
and singular increments of grace, almost
a substance, almost our only friend.

Greatness beyond measure, love
beyond doubt, we wished to bring Him
these
so that we might be once again
like Him and He
like us, mortally awake inside the trouble and beauty
of that burning tree
of which we were not to eat.

To this purpose and this dream
we sought Him all our lives, each
shouldering the extra burdens as others fell away
into the magic of finitude, each
singing Here oh God are the bones
of our brethren, given for thee.
Stretch out thine arms, receive them that they may join with
thee again and all existence be
a single flame.

The Story

We were advised the queen in her turnings
was a necromancy, a spitting crimp
of immemorial mendacity, her beauty
nothing but skin-deep stains,
so they told us, leaning close, denting
their haloes in a rush to offer
the new order conspiracy. Traveler beware,
they said, even the essence of buttercup
she exudes is racks and thumb screws
after dark. It is the *innocent* who shall be
smitten, good people, they said, the heedless
be bent to her poisonous lure. Therefore
we make you a gift, or nearly a gift,
of our queen-proof methodology, all good
and nothing up its sleeve. See?
Oh, we thought, *that* story.

Rachel

It was a small hotel with a stone façade;
or, a hotel with a façade of small stones.
It was late, and difficult to tell.
We beat and beat upon the gate, though the sound
we made was soft as breath
before it stops.

Étienne saw the horses to a nearby shed
and I went in out of the snow.
The hotelier came to where I stood by the fire
and asked would we need the cradle referred to
in the correspondence, and I said no.

After he left to attend our bags, I said it also
to the fire, the lampshade, the brass fittings
on the scuttle. I said it climbing the stairs
and to Étienne later, though
his back was turned and he asleep.

In the morning I said no to the light
as though it had proposed. I said no again
to that poor woman in the mirror, her swollen
breasts and icy, tear-wracked grin.

In the carriage, as we traversed the glittering uplands
north of Besançon, I said no to lust and beauty and
honor and restraint. I saw again
the doctor's funereal trap
clacking slowly down the drive and I said no to that
and then also to the crib and the crying
and the silence after.

Since He was clearly a monster, I said no to God,
felt myself shudder with the power
of that negation, and wondered how much
I might refuse. Perhaps one might, by such refusal,

walk backward on the clock
until the world that had been rises up, new
and undestroyed.
This is why people kill themselves,
I thought.

Sun began to shiver the snowy trees.
We moved along almost without a sound. Once
a crow called. Once the driver
cracked his whip and Étienne, who had been dozing,
stammered what, what, are we there? And I said no,
not quite.

He tells me it was miles before he woke again
and found me gone, the carriage door waving like a wing.

      *   *   *   *

And surely I did fly
into a white blue tower
made of little bones they tell me now was ice.

The woodman found me sitting in a tree
and stiff as frozen cream.
He had to break my arms to get me free.

I had been watching great flights of geese
passing south, calling out like women
crying for some loss.

On the sleigh ride into town I changed myself
so nobody would know I was not there.
Étienne spoke to me from the painful far bank

of a stream.
A boatman with spectacles and a beard
suggested that I cross

and larks of absolution kept urging me to sing.
But I said, no, give me a little more
time.

                *   *   *   *

Then there was too much light
in the room, bits of it
like the room
clung to me as I rose through white glass
of the roof, terrifying
the white-frocked magician, fallen like a tired star
into my sleep.

There was so much light
the creatures in my soul were squinting blind
under its brightness
and over the weeks, or years, sacrificed every lamb they had
that it might let them live.

Stubborn, against even light's most terrible attacks,
they ground their teeth and vowed
to hold fast whatever dark might keep its secret self
in this room, and the next.

And the magician, with his huge eye, kept coming back.

                *   *   *   *

Now bone and mind I am "made whole," they say,
the miracle
clarity of modern understanding having pierced me
to let out all my shadow into light, where, of course,
it simply dissipates.

The Viennese doctor informs
that, though still a woman, I am nearly perfect,
now that I no
longer hate my body, my mother and my dreams, no

longer bring forth in every room that "no," with its zero
at the end opening to swallow my mouth
then everything that is.

       *   *   *   *

At a window in Marseille I stand and watch children
in the street.

They look like roses, bunching and disbursing, an unseen hand,
maybe, among them, making their little stems dance
as if the great and holy day somehow
were theirs alone.

The smokeless burn of happiness ignites in me: how beautiful
to possess such a rose!
I put aside the beads I have been telling and go out with my shears
to set one free.

Three Voice Roulette at Ghostly's

I have thought so many times of her beautiful hair,
he said,
and of how she lay in light like a rose after
the rain,
and of how she moved in the world as though the world
were water
and she perhaps the wind.

He held the gun to his temple and looked up at something
that might have been passing.
Then he said, I saw her once years later in this very bar
she came right out
of a broken juke box and sat beside me and gave me her soft
invisible hands.
Welcome, she said, to the country of glass
estrangement.

Then he had time enough, looking straight
at me, to pull the trigger six times
and put the gun
away. How beautiful she was with that hair shining like dark
silver, he said,
like a nickel-plated loss of meaning with six empty chambers
or a song you play and play
until the juke box breaks and the other customers depart
and the publican
locks up and switches off her bright green eyes.

And she said, so then he just sat there, remembering
        my hair and looking
right where he supposed I might be.
I had the impulse to touch his arm and make him
        cry out and shiver.
But what use? We lose everything, in the end, everything
we had and everything we didn't.
I might have told him that
there is no bourbon in the afterlife, just as in life there is no place
to hide
our pitiful treasures—even when, like me, they don't exist.

Sometimes, he said, I think she still talks about me. I can hear
something
sometimes, after hours when suddenly death's memory leans
against the bar
and writes, *My friend, my beautiful friend,* in the dust
and there's this semblance
of voice
urging an old truth toward the door, which, of course,
is locked.

The Rain Is Not Discouraged

Rain again. Sir Francis Drake
turns up the ruffled collar of his coat.
No bloody chance of a carriage
anywhere in London at this hour.

The dripping feather in his hat
looks like trampled grass extracted
from a hairball or a sump.
He thinks of the Albigensians,
of how they had believed the flesh
evil, particularly when wet.

He notes without surprise an angel
of the Lord beside him, clothed
in a shimmery material
from which the rain simply glances
like peas off of armor plate, and that
he/she/it is lugging a huge basket
of assorted fruit.

For six dark blocks they slosh
in silence, Drake thinking of islands
where it rains only when one dreams of it,
the angel offering pieces of fruit
which the darkness renders unidentifiable.

Sir Francis becomes depressed
and the angel puzzled.
Something else is supposed to happen
but nothing does.
The rain, however, is not discouraged,
it comes down in great armadas,
it comes down like the tears of God.

Bon Voyage

It was the day of paper boats
setting off down the muddy stream
we had created in the driveway.

Made of blue, my boat
breasted ripples of the hose-fed current, spinning
a little in the eddies that formed
at edges of the potholes and moving on bravely
under its napkin sail
upon which I had drawn a Danish flag
in honor of my mother who was
beautiful and knew the Danish word
for that.

I invited her aboard, of course, and our journey
bloomed with the power of time
to stop itself
and come into those who have given over knowledge
in the service of delight.
And when would we have sight of the new land?
And what lay coiled in the dark
beneath us?

Our course set, we stood together, linking
our fingers. Did she see the future?
I let my gaze lift and felt the tangy wind.

PART
III
THE INNER LIFE
[WITH CROWS]

There is no secret contingency.
There's only the rearrangement, the redescription
Of little and mortal things.
There's only this single body, this tiny garment
Gathering the past against itself.
Charles Wright

The Inner Life

At the beginning of Fall,
under the shadow, as they say,
of a blind man's watch,
I open my window
and smell the rain
still two months away
or the rain on my shoulders
when I was a boy
or the rain in my daughter's hair.

In a moment I'll overflow
with sadness again.
But now
I peer down through my skull

to an endless stretch of beach.
Off shore, whale song lifts
against all logic
from the contented anonymity of salt.
Shells gather in waves awash with phlox.
With nowhere to go, I put off
in a boat which must be
the boat of open windows
of the inner life, knowing itself again.

Report from the Empty Room

Hello. Hello. Either you're listening
somewhere, or I'm a fool
            again, tripping on my old tongue tangled
as it is
with this confusion,
            which I confess
is a disguise to keep what's broken
                        from breaking down.
Must be painful, you might say.
Or perhaps you'd try to soothe me by sudden illumination
of that photo of us
            laughing in a park. Or maybe you'd offer, just
on the eye's edge,
            the shadow of a movement
so I could almost know
that you were near.

Anyway, *vie gehts?* as the Deutschlanders say.
Do you have enough to read? Did you get my last
            about the argument I'm having
with God? We disagree
constantly now over the shape and meaning
            of this world
which no longer contains you.
He stays one jump ahead because He's God,
but my new strategy is doubt, which pisses Him
                        no end
and keeps Him too distracted to really
            finish me off.
No news to speak of, I suppose, so
this message is more or less like the others: war and snow
and hunger go on making themselves
                        inside of us
and out. Your brother marches off to school
each day like a soldier
            ordered to clean out a machine gun nest.

At bedtime he prays to dream
of flying with you "above the highest clouds."
Sometimes, like this morning, I open my mouth
and dark comes to ask if this is our only life

or if, in another nearby world, some things
          have found their way into the open light
that brings us home.

"What thou lov'st well remains,
                              the rest is dross
What thou lov'st well shall not be reft from thee"

Thus wrote Pound
in the pit of his grief and shame
and when I read it, I feel huge icebergs breaking up
in my blood.
          And yet it is not so,
or I think that, when, like now, I find myself
                              speaking
into the emptiness of certain rooms.

I don't mean to put you, or God (whom I doubt),
on the spot, but if you could simply graze the least hem
          of my hand
I'd know again what words are for
and the sun would blink and shine out
                              a little
over trees and rooftops of the old life
and things would not seem so bad.

The Refusal to Count Beyond Seven

There were seven crows inside her
gibbering and flapping, emitting
the occasional squawk, much more
like a suddenly discovered moon
than a language.
Sometimes she hopped around
because of this.

At sunset we would find her on the roof
looking for the rest of her clan
or for that Nebraska corresponding
to a crow's curious need for endlessness.

Come down, we said. Or,
keep still. We can help you to realize
the longed for objective world; even a body, perhaps
clothed in the rectitude and amazed glare of those
who have somehow returned to themselves.

We said much the same daily
while the waters rose and dark wings
discovered her shoulder blades
and beaks darted from her mirror-black eyes.
It was all too much for us, her transformation,
her beauty

becoming kiss by kiss a strange wind
or seven strange movements
among and beyond the trees we thought were ours
but would not count.

The Paradox of Place

I'm not sure how I have been
so long like a red kimono in the dark
of a house abandoned, paint
peeling off in scallops and clouds

and the moon comes home
with nothing in its mouth and no one near.

How explain the intricate figure
of absence
to the beloved dead who are now so many.
Do they come back like the moon?

Grass is long and shining by the old truck
I have been driving all my life

on a mountain road, knowing home had
to be somewhere, seeming to remember
a bridge and after that
a path

and then the house that runs on empty
red kimonos, wild
roses where there used to be a door.

Twine

1.

At an edge of the village I remember
birds are twittering confetti
tossed up by the breeze and someone's grandfather
guides a tractor down the broad rows of trees.

Chicken Licken, in that story meant to warn us
about worry, was right: the sky has fallen
even upon the snare and solitude of last year's ploughing.
It is not enough simply to recall

the wet dirt smell of summer air before the rain.

2.

Down at Dickson's, deep in a chocolate phosphate,
the one-time mayor thinks about the beauty of the day
and how the waitress's pastel uniform has just been
washed and starched so that it utters little admiring whispers

when she moves. He draws hard
one last time on the straw and watches her twitching walk
until the glass begins to sputter
and she turns toward him with a faint smile.

After Three Years

The dark branch breaks under a crow
that has been trying to break it.
My daughter's face
fades in and out of the clouds gathered
like sheep
at the end of the day.

I close my eyes. The roses

ask for water
and a map for the oddly familiar aging
man whose features are famished
for someone he used to know.

I go off over the hill of three trees
leaning, like years, with love's intemperance.

My pockets are empty
again.
I hum a tune in case she might be
near enough
to hear as I go along

the path we used to travel, holding our lives
in front of ourselves like
robins' eggs

brought down by wind and still
miraculously unbroken.

Elinor

for Elinor Howell (1919 – 2005)

The tall trees tip their hats
as she is passing.
The berry fields sway from shadows
where they have waited ripe and shining
more than eighty years.
They bend, but what is wind
worth now
that she is passing?
On high the hawk tilts and falls veering
and blue bound as the day itself.
Others enter and depart
along the narrow dusty sunlit road
leading away from time.
Someone beautiful is passing.

The Agnostic Prays for Rain

Outside is dark itself
and things
get small inside the actual
hope and pleasure of them,
which is distance or a voice
thinning as when clouds
forget themselves above a room
for the absentmindedly devout.

Did you follow that? Is it true:
from thin clouds, cold rain?

Rain of shells in the burning house
bending its wing. Rain of memory
among cattails, spatterdock and the marsh
birds
still as stones.
Forgive me, but, are we

alone here? Is there spirit in these
flocks and bones?

Wind off the River Asks if I've Seen Myself
Lately and, if so, Do I Remember the Name

of that girl who gave me a book about Fridtjof Nansen's
courage and the ecstasies of cold?

Face flushed under her light brown hair, she holds out
to me the package wrapped in blue

and the card which, when I read it later, says
"This book made me think of you."

Standing in the hallway, shoulders hunched
as though in fear of a beating, her cheap sweater

slightly askew, she was not beautiful
to me then, was someone I hardly knew.

So I said thanks, wished her, a Jew, Merry Christmas,
and went on home, feeling vaguely

like an undelivered message. And now
it is Christmas again and here is the book

and her face as I turned and left my shadow
shamed and puzzled before her, Christmas music

somewhere in the background, the memory
of her many small gestures toward me

all that year
winking on and off like tiny green and red lights.

And now snow is falling into the black river
and huge silent pines of my neighborhood.

Suddenly, in answer to the wind, I see myself
exiled in the far north of longing. Forsaken

by the crows, I have brought only one book
and I read it again and again.

A Crow's Elegy for the Farmer's Daughter

We gathered in the fern-thin treetops at dusk
or in the flat sear of noon
strutted among puddles and spoke only
of the sky's empty torment
or ourselves. Once in awhile

we flapped in the dust and silver rain
and disparaged wind with our bevel-winged plummetings
and soundless glides.
We did not care
who shot at us for our raucous predawn menacing
or for settling like a plague of black books in fields
under the blindness of those homespun effigies
leering and motionless and coming unstuffed.

We did not care for you
though we saw the cortege winding past the arbor
and drunken berry rows, the ghosts of peach trees bowing
to acknowledge death's grand simplicity at last
revealed.

We were pieces of a blackboard
upon which last rites were written and did not care
who could or could not see
that we were gods and you were not
ever coming home,

in spite of the mourners' deeply foolish love
we could imagine only by flying
into the sun, where every grief is charred
and finally burned away.

Cascade

Harold Godwin died with an arrow in his eye and his lady, Eadgyth of the Swan-Neck, beaten and raped and raped again, sent their children into the north where they died of safekeeping.

Thus ended the line of Godwin kings, one king long.

Thus ended the shield wall of theyns at Hastings, butchered every one upon the feast of St. Josephine, patron of confused boys and older women.

Thus ended English as a variant of Norse.

Thus were Arthur and Boadecea avenged and Robin Hood's green shadow born amongst the future trees.

Thus was the empire wrung from the farm, the Irish trampled and dispossessed for three hundred years.

Thus were the incomparable Shakespeare and Sir Thomas More and the great white queen who removed her cousin's head, though she did not want to.

Thus were the tall ships and Australia and the opium trade.

Thus was the Northwest Passage, never found.

Thus was America and Jefferson, Lincoln and Custer.

Thus were the bones of buffalo scattered numberless over the land like a ruin of whitened pianos.

Thus were Carrie Nation and the Brooklyn Bridge and the Volstead Act.

Thus might both my children have someday looked back at Harold, rushing his army up the road to Stamford Bridge to fight his turncoat brother and Hardrada's northmen then turning back in forced marches half the length of England to meet William. Thus might they have loved him, as I do, for his courage and for whatever might have been.

De Pictura

The *Axis Visualis* is not the whole field
of view. Beyond the central tree
three crows are peripheral and forgotten
by the man seeking a way out
of the painting on my wall.
You might say the "eye of the mind"
insists, with Plato, that light is knowledge,
that the crows, being black, are nothing
known and therefore possibly in league
with that darkened fountain at the heart of all
intimations of loss.

Meanwhile, the man and I are non-
transactional, since for two hundred years
now he is turned away, falsely brightened
by what he already knows: the way out

is that point of vanishment where mirrors
devour themselves and light's purity
is blind as a bricked-in lamp.
So I can't help his grey and blue form
turn left and climb the stair
as I could not help my grandfather
unplatonically collapsed
on the kitchen floor, his spirit passing
over my shoulder to a field with one
bent tree and three crows
in the perfect stillness of flight.

Una Furtiva Lagrima

I guess I was thinking of the sea
when night is upon it
and the stars converse with the phosphorus
and sharks rise toward the moon.
I guess I was by myself in the old garage
with the tractor and the smell of dust
and harness with walnuts striking
the flat roof like meditative hammers.
I guess I was remembering a rocky riverbank
and a woman unclothed in gold
dazzles of desire
and how at last it went so bad
and how crows glistening with rain
flock to a particular otherwise forgotten tree.
I guess I was back on the mound, about to throw
the third strike that would seal the no-hitter
and everyone would yell and jump around
as though I had saved a life or given myself
to something beautiful that had been
about to leave us forever.
Or I was thinking of wind in bare branches
of our last peach tree dying and dreaming
of its orchard and the smell of dirt and leaves.
I guess I was thinking of the dispassionate
almost careless sea as it breaks and drags things off
and casts them back, returning whatever loneliness
had brought them there and writing their names
in a book everyone has been saving to buy.
I guess I was a spire of far-off bones
with the rain and crows inside it,
and the child was lost.

The Mystery of Names

Once on New Year's I woke alone before dawn
in a house where I had been
to a party. Everyone,
including those whose house it was,
had gone off and left me asleep in a chair
in the living room with the front door open and rain
blowing in.

The house was very still. I saw blearily
reflected in dark windows the solemn glass
faces of the dead
as they passed into grey boats and set out toward
darkly distant harbors edged with light.

I was young. None of this transport
had yet occurred for those I loved. Nevertheless
I was certain such boats would bear us all, eventually,
with equal sureness.

After awhile I heard my name
and went out onto the empty porch
and looked down on Arthur Street, bright
as hammered pewter,
and saw, farther on, the actual river
stippled and glittering with light from the houseboats.

Some few times we are given to know our lives are nothing
but themselves, that they mean
themselves, that they are not biography or myth
or platonic apotheosis. But

in this knowledge is the mystery of names
and faces
and the dead who have left us
sleeping, dreaming this moment and the next
until we wake, as I did, and walk home in the rain.

I Wake Again

I woke beside the billowing angel bodies
of the curtains
in that room where, years before, someone completely dear to me
had liked to dwell
in the dense light and blindness of life's morning.

Then I woke again and she was that distant nameless thing,
a waterfall or mountain,
perhaps a shaft of light on one of these.

Who's to say, when someone turns to time and waking
becomes the dream
bitterly unbelievable in its absolute nature, its hills
unfamiliar
as the road winding away through them?

When I woke again, flags were flying. Far off
band music insisted.
Outside, the birds leapt into rain and fluttered down like blossoms
blown off course.
I woke again and again in the strangely empty house.

Listen

Is it an empty house, the body alone
with its weary old clothes
or its bullet holes and severed arteries,
last laugh still shining in its teeth?

The road of answers leaps its ditch
and descends a dusty hollow
where nightbirds coo, *Pass by,* and the Angel
of Nothingness does his nails.

Often sky dazzles
over the great breathing earth.
Often of its own accord the grain begins again
to simmer. Deep in the dark

I find my wife's hand and listen
as the blue trees bow and bend and I want my soul
to tell about itself almost
anything.

And it says *I, too, am a traveler.*
Wait for me.

Christopher Howell is the author of ten collections of poems, most recently *Dreamless and Possible: Poems New and Selected* (2010) and *Light's Ladder* (2004), both from the University of Washington Press. His poems, translations, and essays have appeared widely in anthologies and journals including *Antioch Review, Colorado Review, Crazyhorse, Southern Review, Iowa Review,* and *Harper's.* He has been the recipient of numerous awards for his work, among them, four Pushcart Prizes and two fellowships from the National Endowment for the Arts. Howell lives in Spokane, where he teaches at Eastern Washington University. He is also director and principal editor for Lynx House Press.

PHOTO BY MATTHEW VALENTINE

More Poetry from Milkweed Editions

To order books or for more information, contact Milkweed at
(800) 520-6455
or visit our Web site (www.milkweed.org).

The City, Our City
By Wayne Miller

What have you done to our ears to make us hear echoes?
By Arlene Kim

The Nine Senses
By Melissa Kwasny

Sharks in the Rivers
By Ada Limón

Fancy Beasts
By Alex Lemon

Seedlip and Sweet Apple
By Arra Lynn Ross

Milkweed Editions

Founded as a nonprofit organization in 1980, Milkweed Editions is an independent publisher. Our mission is to identify, nurture and publish transformative literature, and build an engaged community around it.

Join Us

In addition to revenue generated by the sales of books we publish, Milkweed Editions depends on the generosity of institutions and individuals like you. In an increasingly consolidated and bottom-line-driven publishing world, your support allows us to select and publish books on the basis of their literary quality and transformative potential. Please visit our Web site (www.milkweed.org) or contact us at (800) 520-6455 to learn more.

Milkweed Editions, a nonprofit publisher, gratefully acknowledges sustaining support from the following:

Maurice and Sally Blanks
Emilie and Henry Buchwald
The Bush Foundation
The Patrick and Aimee Butler
    Foundation
Timothy and Tara Clark
Betsy and Edward Cussler
The Dougherty Family
    Foundation
Julie B. DuBois
John and Joanne Gordon
Ellen Grace
William and Jeanne Grandy
John and Andrea Gulla
The Jerome Foundation
The Lerner Foundation
The Lindquist & Vennum
    Foundation
Sanders and Tasha Marvin
The McKnight Foundation
Mid-Continent Engineering
The Minnesota State Arts
    Board, through an
    appropriation by The
    Minnesota State Legislature
    and a grant from The
    National Endowment for
    The Arts
Kelly Morrison and John
    Willoughby
The National Endowment for
    The Arts
The Navarre Corporation
Ann and Doug Ness

Jörg and Angie Pierach
The RBC Foundation USA
Pete Rainey
Deborah Reynolds
Cheryl Ryland
Schele and Philip Smith
The Target Foundation
The Travelers Foundation
Moira and John Turner
Edward and Jenny Wahl.

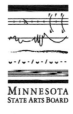

ART WORKS.
arts.gov

CLEAN
WATER
LAND &
LEGACY
AMENDMENT

MINNESOTA
STATE ARTS BOARD

BUSH
FOUNDATION

TARGET.

Interior design by Hopkins/Baumann
Typeset in Bertold Garamond
by Will Hopkins
Printed on acid-free 30%
postconsumer waste paper
by BookMobile